COOKIES
Cook Books from Amish Kitchens

Phyllis Pellman Good • Rachel Thomas Pellman

Good Books
Intercourse, PA 17534
800/762-7171
www.GoodBooks.com

COOKIES
Cook Books from Amish Kitchens

What simpler pleasure than a warm, freshly baked cookie? And with the best cookies go memories...

"Grandma always let me put the raisins on the sugar cookies she baked for market..." These recipes are favorites, most of them several generations old!

Cover art and design by Cheryl A. Benner.
Design and art in body by Craig N. Heisey; Calligraphy by Gayle Smoker.
This special edition is an adaptation of *Cookies: From Amish and Mennonite Kitchens, Pennsylvania Dutch Cookbooks*, and from *Cook Books by Good Books*.
Copyright © 1983, 1991, 1996 by Good Books, Intercourse, PA 17534.
ISBN: 978-1-56148-193-4. All rights reserved. Printed in the United States of America.

Contents

Chocolate Chip Cookies	4
Soft Raisin Cookies	5
Amish Cookies	6
Hermits	7
Date Balls	8
Snickerdoodles	8
Shrewberry Cookies	9
Peanut Butter Cookies	10
Oatmeal Peanut Butter Cookies	11
Filled Oatmeal Cookies	12
Oatmeal Cookies	13
Oatmeal Whoopie Pies	14
Chocolate Whoopie Pies	15
Pumpkin Whoopie Pies	16
Gingersnaps	17
Gingerbread Men	18
Ginger Cookies	19
Caramel Cookies	20
Brown Sugar Cookies	20
Molasses Cookies	21
Aunt Carrie's Butterscotch Ice-Box Cookies	22
Sand Tarts	23
Drop Sugar Cookies	24
Fudge-Nut Cookies	25
Fresh Glazed Apple Cookies	26
Walnut Supreme Cookies	27
Golden Nuggets	28
Applesauce Nuggets	29
Boston Fruit Cookies	30
Cherry Winks	31
Pecan Tassies	32

Chocolate Chip Cookies

    1 cup shortening   Makes about 8 dozen
    2 cups sugar
    4 eggs
    1 cup sour cream
    4 cups flour
    ½ tsp. salt
    2 tsp. soda
    1 or 2 packs chocolate chips
    1 cup chopped nuts
    2 cups raisins (boiled, cooled, and drained), optional

1. Cream shortening and sugar.
2. Add eggs and beat till fluffy. Add sour cream and mix well. Gradually add flour, salt, and soda. Mix well.
3. Stir in chocolate chips, nuts, and raisins, if desired.
4. Drop by heaping teaspoons onto greased cookie sheet. Bake at 375° for 10 minutes.

    They are more moist when they are kept in the freezer a while.
    "The most delicious cookies I've ever made! They taste more-ish. I didn't get a chance to put any in the freezer."

Soft Raisin Cookies

Makes about 9 dozen

- 2 cups raisins
- 1 cup boiling water
- 3/4 cup shortening
- 2 cups sugar
- 3 eggs
- 1 tsp. vanilla
- 4 cups flour
- 1 tsp. baking powder
- 1 tsp. baking soda
- 1 tsp. salt
- 1 tsp. cinnamon
- 1/4 tsp. cloves
- 1/4 tsp. nutmeg
- 1 cup chopped nuts

1. Add boiling water to raisins. Cook 5 minutes. Set aside to cool.
2. Cream shortening and sugar. Add eggs and vanilla and beat well.
3. Sift together flour, baking powder, baking soda, salt, and spices. Add alternately with raisin liquid to creamed mixture. Stir in raisins and nuts.
4. Chill dough for several hours or overnight.
5. Drop by teaspoons onto greased cookie sheet. Bake at 350° for about 12 minutes.

Amish Cookies

Makes 7½ dozen

2½ cups sugar
1⅛ cups shortening
3 eggs
⅔ cup dark molasses
1 cup sour milk
6½ cups flour
2 Tbsp. baking powder
3 Tbsp. cinnamon
2 Tbsp. soda
1½ tsp. nutmeg
2 cups oatmeal
1 cup raisins
¾ cup chopped peanuts or walnuts

1. Cream sugar and shortening. Add eggs and beat well.
2. Add milk and molasses alternately with sifted dry ingredients.
3. Add oatmeal, raisins, and nuts. Mix with hands. Bake at 350° for 8-10 minutes.

Hermits

1 cup shortening
1 cup sugar
1 cup brown sugar
4 eggs
½ cup molasses
1 tsp. baking soda dissolved in
½ cup warm water
4½ cups flour
¼ tsp. salt
½ tsp. ground cloves
1 cup chopped nuts
1 cup chopped dates

Makes about 10 dozen

1. Cream shortening and sugars.
2. Add eggs and beat until light and fluffy.
3. Sift dry ingredients and add alternately with water and molasses. Beat after each addition.
4. Stir in chopped nuts and dates.
5. Drop by rounded teaspoons onto greased cookie sheet. Bake at 350° for 10-12 minutes.

Variation:
   Use ½ cup cooled black coffee instead of water. Add 1 cup raisins and 1 cup chopped dried apricots in place of nuts and dates.

Date Balls

    1 cup sugar   Makes 3 dozen
    ½ cup butter
    dash of salt
    1 cup chopped dates
    1 egg, beaten
    1 cup chopped pecans
    2 cups Rice Krispies cereal
    coconut

1. Heat first three ingredients over low heat until butter is melted.
2. Add dates and beaten egg and bring to boil. Boil 5 minutes, stirring constantly.
3. Cool. Add pecans and cereal. Form balls 1½ inch in diameter. Roll in coconut.

Snickerdoodles

    1 cup shortening   Makes 4 dozen
    1½ cups sugar
    2 eggs
    2¾ cups flour
    2 tsp. cream of tartar
    1 tsp. soda
    ½ tsp. salt

1. Cream shortening and sugar. Add eggs and beat well.
2. Sift together flour, cream of tartar, soda, and salt. Gradually stir into creamed mixture.
3. Chill dough 2 hours or more. Form into balls the size of walnuts. Roll each ball in a mixture of 2 Tbsp. sugar and 2 tsp. cinnamon. Bake at 400° for about 10 minutes. (Cookies should be lightly browned but still soft.)

Shrewberry Cookies

2¼ cups brown sugar   Makes 6 dozen
¾ cup shortening
4 eggs
4 cups flour
1 tsp. soda
1 tsp. nutmeg
1 tsp. cinnamon
1 tsp. cloves

1. Cream sugar and shortening. Add eggs and beat well.
2. Add flour, soda, and spices and mix well.
3. Drop by rounded teaspoons onto cookie sheet. Sprinkle with sugar. Bake at 375° for 10-12 minutes.

Peanut Butter Cookies

Makes 5 dozen

1 cup sugar
1 cup brown sugar
1 cup butter
1 cup shortening
1 cup peanut butter
2 eggs
1 tsp. soda
½ tsp. salt
1 tsp. vanilla
3 cups flour

1. Cream sugars and shortening. Add peanut butter and mix well. Add eggs and mix well.
2. Add soda, salt, and vanilla. Gradually add flour.
3. Roll into balls and place 2 inches apart on cookie sheet. Flatten balls with fork dipped in flour to prevent sticking. Bake at 375° for 10-12 minutes.

"So buttery they melt in your mouth!"

Oatmeal Peanut Butter Cookies

Makes 5½ dozen

1 cup sugar
1 cup brown sugar
1 cup shortening
1 cup peanut butter
3 eggs
1½ cups flour
1 tsp. soda
1 tsp. salt
1 tsp. vanilla
2 cups quick oats
1 cup chocolate morsels or raisins

1. Cream sugars and shortening. Add eggs and peanut butter and beat well.
2. Gradually add flour, salt, and soda. Add vanilla. Stir in quick oats and chocolate morsels or raisins.
3. Drop by heaping teaspoons onto cookie sheet. Bake at 350° for 15 minutes.

"These cookies disappear fast. They're like 2 good cookies in 1."

Filled Oatmeal Cookies

1 cup sugar　　　　　　　　　　Makes 3 dozen
1 cup shortening
2 cups oatmeal (grind in blender)
2 cups flour
½ tsp. soda
½ tsp. salt
½ cup sour milk

1. Cream sugar and shortening.
2. Combine dry ingredients and add alternately with sour milk. Mix well.
3. Roll ¼-½ inch thick on floured board. Cut with round cookie cutter and bake at 350° for 10-12 minutes.

Filling

1 cup sugar
1 cup water
2 cups dates (ground or finely chopped)

1. Combine ingredients in saucepan and cook 20-30 minutes until thickened.
2. Place a spoonful of filling between 2 cookies and press firmly together.

Variation:

Sweet milk may be used in place of sour milk. Omit baking soda and add 3 tsp. baking powder.

Oatmeal Cookies

1 cup brown sugar Makes 5 dozen
½ cup sugar
¾ cup shortening
1 egg
¼ cup water
1 tsp. vanilla
1 tsp. salt
½ tsp. soda
1½ cups flour
3 cups oats (old fashioned or quick cooking)

1. Cream sugars and shortening. Add egg, water, and vanilla and beat until creamy.
2. Sift together flour, soda, and salt and add to creamed mixture. Mix well. Stir in oats.
3. Drop by heaping teaspoons onto greased cookie sheet. Bake at 350° for 10-15 minutes.

Variation:

Chopped nuts, raisins, chocolate chips, or coconut may also be added.

Oatmeal Whoopie Pies

2 cups brown sugar
¾ cup butter or shortening
2 eggs
½ tsp. salt
1 tsp. cinnamon
1 tsp. baking powder
3 Tbsp. boiling water
1 tsp. soda
2 ½ cups flour
2 cups oatmeal

Makes 3 dozen sandwich pies

1. Cream sugar and shortening.
2. Add eggs; then add salt, cinnamon, and baking powder. Add soda dissolved in hot water. Gradually add flour and oatmeal.
3. Drop batter by heaping teaspoons onto greased cookie sheet. Bake at 350° for 8-10 minutes or until brown.

Filling

1 egg white, beaten
2 Tbsp. milk
1 tsp. vanilla
1 cup 10x sugar

1. Mix; then add one more cup 10x sugar and ¾ cup shortening.

2. Spread dab of filling on flat side of cooled cookie. Top with another cookie to form a sandwich pie.

Chocolate Whoopie Pies

2 cups sugar
1 cup shortening
2 eggs
4 cups flour
1 cup baking cocoa
2 tsp. vanilla
1 tsp. salt
1 cup sour milk
2 tsp. baking soda
1 cup hot water

Makes 4 dozen sandwich pies

1. Cream sugar and shortening. Add eggs.
2. Sift together flour, cocoa, and salt. Add alternately with sour milk. Add vanilla. Dissolve soda in hot water and add last. Mix well.
3. Drop by rounded teaspoons onto cookie sheet. Bake at 400° for 8-10 minutes.
4. Make sandwiches from 2 cookies filled with Whoopie Pie Filling. Recipe for filling will need to be doubled for this batch of cookies (see page 14).

Pumpkin Whoopie Pies

2 cups brown sugar
1 cup vegetable oil
1½ cups cooked, mashed pumpkin
2 eggs
3 cups flour
1 tsp. salt
1 tsp. baking powder
1 tsp. baking soda
1 tsp. vanilla
1½ Tbsp. cinnamon
½ Tbsp. ginger
½ Tbsp. ground cloves

Makes 3 dozen sandwich pies

1. Cream sugar and oil.
2. Add pumpkin and eggs. Add flour, salt, baking powder, soda, vanilla, and spices. Mix well.
3. Drop by heaping teaspoons onto greased cookie sheet. Bake at 350° for 10-12 minutes.
4. Make sandwiches from 2 cookies filled with the Whoopie Pie Filling recipe on page 14.

Variation:
   Adding ½ cup black walnuts (ground) gives these cookies a special delicious flavor.

Gingersnaps

3 cups sugar
2¼ cups shortening
3 eggs
¾ cup molasses
3 Tbsp. ground ginger
3 tsp. cinnamon
6 tsp. baking soda
1½ tsp. salt
6½ cups flour

Makes 11 dozen

1. Cream sugar and shortening. Add eggs and molasses and beat well. Add spices, soda, and salt. Mix well.
2. Gradually add flour. Dough will become very stiff and may need to be mixed by hand.
3. Form 1 inch balls from dough. Roll each ball in sugar and place 2 inches apart on cookie sheet. Do not flatten. Bake at 350° for 12-15 minutes.

"They should not be overly brown when you take them out of the oven, and will be puffed up a bit, but will get 'snappy' when cooled."

Gingerbread Men

1 cup margarine   Makes 3 dozen
1 cup sugar
½ cup dark molasses
1 tsp. cinnamon
1 tsp. nutmeg
1 tsp. cloves
1 tsp. ginger
2 eggs
1 tsp. vinegar
5 cups flour
1 tsp. baking soda
raisins and cinnamon candies

1. In saucepan cream margarine and sugar. Add molasses and spices. Mix well. Bring to boil, constantly stirring. Remove from heat and cool.
2. Stir in well-beaten eggs and vinegar. Sift flour and baking soda and stir into molasses mixture to form a smooth dough.
3. Chill several hours. Divide dough into 6 portions. Roll out on aluminum foil. Cut with gingerbread man cutter. Remove excess dough. Garnish with raisins for eyes and buttons and cinnamon candies for mouth.
4. Place foil and men on cookie sheet and bake at 350° for 8-10 minutes.

Ginger Cookies

1 cup dark brown sugar   Makes 4½ dozen
½ cup shortening
1 egg
½ cup Brer Rabbit molasses
1 tsp. ginger
1½ tsp. cinnamon
3 cups flour
½ tsp. salt
1½ tsp. soda
1 cup sour milk
½ tsp. vanilla

1. Cream sugar and shortening. Add egg, molasses, ginger, and cinnamon.
2. Sift flour, soda, and salt. Add alternately with sour milk. Add vanilla. Chill dough several hours.
3. Drop by teaspoons onto cookie sheet. Bake at 400° for 6-8 minutes.

"I bake these at Christmas and sprinkle red and green sugar on top."

Caramel Cookies

2 cups brown sugar   Makes 5½ dozen
½ cup butter
½ cup shortening
2 eggs
3 cups flour
½ tsp. soda
1 tsp. cream of tartar
¼ tsp. nutmeg
1 Tbsp. water
1 tsp. vanilla

1. Cream sugar, butter, and shortening. Add eggs and beat until light and fluffy.
2. Sift and add dry ingredients. Add water and vanilla.
3. Divide dough in half and form two rolls. Chill overnight. Slice cookies ½ inch thick. Bake at 350° for 10-12 minutes.

Brown Sugar Cookies

2¼ cups brown sugar   Makes 9 dozen
1 cup margarine or shortening
3 eggs
1 tsp. soda
1 tsp. cinnamon
4 cups flour

1. Cream sugar and margarine. Add eggs and beat well.
2. Add soda, cinnamon, and flour. Mix well and chill for several hours.
3. Roll thinly on floured board and cut with cookie cutters. Bake at 350° for 7-8 minutes.

Molasses Cookies

1 cup shortening   Makes 8 dozen
½ lb. light brown sugar
1 pint dark baking molasses
1 pint buttermilk
6 cups flour
1 Tbsp. baking soda

1. Cream shortening and sugar. Add molasses and buttermilk.
2. Stir in flour and baking soda.
3. Drop in large dollops from teaspoon onto cookie sheet. Bake at 375° for 8-10 minutes.

Variation:
    Cookies may be glazed by brushing tops with egg yolk before baking.
    Add 1 tsp. ginger and 1 tsp. cinnamon with flour and soda.

Aunt Carrie's Butterscotch Ice-Box Cookies

1 cup butter   Makes 7 dozen
1 cup brown sugar
2 eggs
3½ cups flour
1 tsp. soda
1 tsp. cream of tartar
1 cup chopped dates
1 cup chopped nuts

1. Cream butter and sugar. Add eggs and beat well.
2. Sift dry ingredients together and gradually add to creamed mixture. Blend well. Stir in chopped dates and nuts.
3. Form into rolls on a platter. Cover and refrigerate overnight. Slice thin and bake at 400° for 8-10 minutes.

Short'nin' Bread Cookies

4 cups flour (sifted)   Makes 2½ dozen
dash of salt
1 cup brown sugar
2 cups butter

1. Combine flour, salt, and sugar. Mix well.
2. Cut in butter until mixture resembles fine crumbs. Work together by hand until dough forms a ball.
3. Pat or roll out ½ inch thick on lightly floured board. Cut circles with 2 inch cookie cutter. Bake at 350° for 20-25 minutes.

Sand Tarts

2 cups sugar
1 cup butter
2 eggs
4 cups flour

Makes 10 dozen

1 Cream sugar, butter, and eggs.
2. Blend in flour.
3. Roll dough very thin and cut in decorative shapes with cookie cutters. Brush top of cookies with egg white and sprinkle with colored sugar or crushed peanuts. Bake at 350° for 8-10 minutes.

Note:
  Do not substitute other shortenings for butter.

Drop Sugar Cookies

1½ cups sugar   Makes 5 dozen
1 cup margarine
2 eggs
1 cup buttermilk or sour cream
3¾ cups flour
2 tsp. baking powder
1 tsp. soda
1 tsp. vanilla

1. Cream sugar and shortening. Add eggs and beat well.
2. Add milk, dry ingredients, and vanilla and mix thoroughly.
3. Drop by teaspoons onto greased cookie sheet. Bake at 375° for 8-10 minutes.

Variation:
    Use 1 tsp. lemon extract in place of vanilla.
    Place a raisin in the center and sprinkle the top of each cookie with sugar before baking.

"Grandma always baked these to sell on market. I was glad when one broke in her box — she'd give it to me to eat!"

Fudge Nut Cookies

1⅔ cup sugar
⅔ cup butter
2 eggs
1 cup cottage cheese
2 tsp. vanilla
2¾ cups flour
½ cup cocoa
1 tsp. baking powder
½ tsp. baking soda
½ tsp. salt
½ cup chopped nuts

Makes 5½ dozen

1. Cream sugar, butter, eggs, and cottage cheese.
2. Add vanilla and dry ingredients. Stir in chopped nuts. Chill dough 2 hours.
3. Roll dough into balls the size of a walnut. Dip in granulated or powdered sugar. Place 2 inches apart on cookie sheet and bake at 350° for 8-10 minutes.

"Good and chocolate-y!"

Fresh Glazed Apple Cookies

1⅓ cup brown sugar   Makes 4½ dozen
½ cup shortening
1 egg
2 cups flour
1 tsp. soda
½ tsp. salt
1 tsp. cinnamon
1 tsp. ground cloves
½ tsp. nutmeg
½ cup milk
1 cup apples (finely chopped, unpared)
1 cup raisins
1 cup nuts

1. Cream sugar and shortening. Add egg and beat well.
2. Add dry ingredients alternately with milk. Stir in apples, raisins, and nuts.
3. Drop by teaspoons onto cookie sheet. Bake at 350° for 12-15 minutes.

Glaze

1½ cups 10x sugar
2½ Tbsp. apple juice or milk
½ tsp. salt

¼ tsp. vanilla
1 Tbsp. butter

1. Cream butter. Gradually add sugar, juice or milk, salt, and vanilla. Beat until smooth.
2. Spread on top of Apple Cookies.

Walnut Supreme Cookies

1 cup sugar　　　　　　　Makes about 6 dozen
1 cup brown sugar
1 cup margarine
3 eggs
3½ cups flour
1 tsp. soda
2 tsp. baking powder
1 cup buttermilk
1 cup chopped walnuts

1. Cream sugars, shortening, and eggs.
2. Sift dry ingredients and add alternately with buttermilk. Fold in chopped nuts.
3. Drop by rounded teaspoons onto greased cookie sheet. Bake at 375° for 8-10 minutes.

Variation:
　After cooling cookies may be frosted with a butter frosting.

Golden Nuggets

½ cup sugar
¼ cup brown sugar
¾ cup shortening
1 egg
2 cups flour
1½ tsp. baking powder
½ tsp. salt
1 cup cooked, mashed carrots
1 tsp. vanilla
1 cup chopped walnuts

Makes 4 dozen

1. Cream sugars and shortening. Add egg, well beaten.
2. Sift dry ingredients together and add alternately with mashed carrots. Add vanilla. Stir in chopped walnuts.
3. Drop by rounded teaspoons onto greased cookie sheet. Bake at 400° for 8-10 minutes.
4. Frost with orange icing while warm.

Orange Icing

1 cup 10x sugar
2 tsp. grated orange rind
2 Tbsp. orange juice
Mix until smooth.

Applesauce Nuggets

1 cup brown sugar　　　　Makes 3½ dozen
½ cup shortening
1 egg
1 cup applesauce
2 cups flour
½ tsp. salt
1 tsp. soda
½ tsp. cinnamon
¼ tsp. cloves
½ tsp. allspice
½ tsp. nutmeg
½ cup chopped pecans
1 cup butterscotch pieces

1. Cream sugar and shortening. Add egg and applesauce and beat well.
2. Sift together flour, salt, soda, and spices. Stir into creamed mixture.
3. Stir in chopped pecans and butterscotch pieces.
4. Drop by heaping teaspoons onto greased cookie sheet. Bake at 375° for 10-12 minutes.

Boston Fruit Cookies

    1½ cups brown sugar   Makes 5 dozen
    1 cup shortening
    3 eggs
    3½ cups flour
    pinch of salt
    1 tsp. soda dissolved in
    ½ cup raisin juice
    1 cup coconut
    1 15 oz. box raisins (boiled, cooled, and drained)

1. Cream sugar and shortening. Add eggs and beat well.
2. Add flour, salt, and soda dissolved in raisin juice. Mix well.
3. Stir in coconut and raisins.
4. Drop by teaspoonfuls onto cookie sheet. Bake at 350° for 8-10 minutes.

Snowballs

    1 cup soft butter   Makes 4 dozen
    ½ cup sifted 10x sugar
    1 tsp. vanilla
    2¼ cups sifted flour
    ¼ tsp. salt
    ¾ cup ground nuts, chilled

1. Cream together butter, sugar, and vanilla.
2. Add flour, salt, and nuts.
3. Roll into 1 inch balls.
4. Place on ungreased cookie sheet.
5. Bake at 400° for 10-12 minutes until set.
6. While still warm, roll in 10x sugar. Cool. Roll in sugar again.

Cherry Winks

Makes 7 dozen

    1 cup sugar
    ¾ cup shortening
    2 eggs
    2 Tbsp. milk
    1 tsp. vanilla
    1 cup chopped nuts
    1 cup chopped dates
    2¼ cups flour
    1 tsp. baking powder
    ½ tsp. salt
    ½ tsp. soda

1. Cream shortening and sugar. Add eggs, milk, vanilla, nuts, and dates.
2. Sift and add dry ingredients.
3. Form balls the size of a walnut. Roll in crushed corn flakes. Flatten slightly and top with half of a maraschino cherry. Bake at 375° for 10-12 minutes.

Pecan Tassies (Tiny Pecan Pies)

½ cup butter or margarine   Makes 2 dozen
3 oz. cream cheese
1 cup flour
¾ cup brown sugar
1 egg
1 Tbsp. butter or margarine
1 tsp. vanilla
dash of salt
⅔ cup pecans, coarsely broken

1. Blend together softened butter or margarine and cream cheese. Stir in flour. Chill dough about 1 hour.
2. Shape dough into 2 dozen 1 inch balls. Place in ungreased 1¾ inch muffin pans. Press dough evenly against sides and bottom of each muffin cup.
3. Blend together brown sugar, egg, butter or margarine, vanilla, and salt. Beat just until smooth.
4. Divide half of the pecans among pastry lined muffin cups. Add egg mixture and top with remaining pecans. Bake at 325° for 25 minutes or until filling is set.
5. Cool before removing from pans.